RESPICE
FINEM

Piper Lawson

ISBN 978-1-63784-397-0 (paperback)
ISBN 978-1-63784-398-7 (digital)

Hawes & Jenkins Publishing
16427 N Scottsdale Road Suite 410
Scottsdale, AZ 85254
www.hawesjenkins.com

Printed in the United States of America

To the brightest star in the sky. Thank you for being my biggest supporter, even though you are no longer here.

To my dad, who always pushes me to the best I can be.

To my sisters—Ryanne, Aspen, and Stormy. Thank you for being my best friends and supporting me always.

To Nikki, who taught me forgiveness heals.

To my grandparents, thank you for supporting me, even though you had no idea I was writing this book.

CONTENTS

Part 2:
Antiqui colant antiquum dierum
"Let the ancients worship the ancient of days"

Part 3:
Ab aeterno:
"From the Eternal"

PREFACE

Morality

I am not a God
    Nor am I a king
I am not a Beast
    Nor am I the Hero
I am simply nothing but a man
    That trembles at the sight
    Of my own mortality
Simply lost in time
    Hollowed by fate
The ice breaks under the weight
    Of my feet
Shadows of the naked oak
    Coats the lake
    On which I stand
Whom am I to breath
    The frigid air that kills my lungs
    In my time of great despair
Chapped lips to speak
    The worlds of truth outloud
    To the infinity unknown

Pain that invades my chest
    Petals falling from my flower

Crimson growing in the
Pure white snow

Cool air surround me
    The fog glides in
    Waltzing gracefully
    In one final dance
Imprisoning me in my
    Final grave
    For I am not more

PART 1:

Ab antiquo:
"From the Ancient"

HOPE

As the sun sinks
    into the eternal horizon
    hope seems to fade
    We chase after it
Long after the moon
    has taken its rightful place
    cascading the heavenly night sky
    in her silver glow
Like Achilles wandering the Earth
    we search for our purpose
    the thing that we hold dear
Fighting the creatures of the World
    and the monsters inside our mind
    we think all is lost
Though malevolent shadows follow us
    and winds of unknown forces
    toss us around
    in a whirlwind of our own emotion
    preying on our fears,
    hoping to capture
    our hearts in their traps;
    and that we will be thrown
    off our course
Waiting until we declare defeat
    and that we feel
    we are too far gone
    to be saved
A beacon of light shines

through the storm
Illuminating the battlefield
We stand tall in the battlefield till this nightmare
is no more
cause the light we have been searching
for, is upon us
We follow it
through harsh winds and deserts
through treacherous plains of the abyss
It always keeps us safe
never letting the night consume us
And as the sun rises again
awakening the Earth from her slumber
the treasure we thought was lost
Is found

THE WORLD

In the brink of hell
  I stood fast against
  The world
Held my ground
  As thousands charged
  At me, ready to kill
I knew the odds
  Were against me
That I might lose
  But I held strong
  And never gave up hope
For I knew you
  Were with me
So I feared no evil
  No army
  I knew you'd save me

MOON ON A
STARLESS NIGHT

Spent the day looking out the window
    watching as life passed by
    Feeling so hollow inside.
    I'm stuck in this trance,
    as if I can't move forward.
How can you move forward,
    when you've lost myself.

These days its getting harder
    to handle it all.
This rain cloud still follows me around.

Feel like the moon
    on a starless night
    or a flower
    in an ocean of weeds.

DESTINY

I know there's been troubles and bad times
    Happiness seems to come and go
    Always searching for a better life
    but having you by my side
    is truly a miracle

It is not going to be
    a smooth path
We both know that life has obstacles
    That life has trials

Growing up is hard
    letting go of the past
    is a game in itself

The darkness of the day
    may wither your flower,
    might destroy your dreams
But even if the world
    crumbles around you
Even if the sun
    grows cold
Believe in the journey

The night only lasts
    so long
So make a wish
    it's your destiny

THE TALE OF DEATH

From the light
We were created
A momentary piece of the
Art of existence
A fragment of the masterpiece that was formed

As we breathed, we lived
Like the trees of the earth
The swans of the lakes
Living to see all, experience all
To love, to find comfort
That one has never experienced

Yet as we grew
The heart began to fade
The rivers slowed
Time sped up
And the world crumbled

The anger of ones soul
Was like a never ending war
Filled with pain, love, frustration
Until it was too much to handle
And no one ever needed to stop
And think
Before choosing the path at the fork
In the road

And there you stood
Like a fading star
That is seen by one who was waiting
For memories
Of the ones shared long ago

Trembling as a sequence of memories
Flooded the mind
The plunging wave of emotions
Hitting the soul
Like a bullet from a gun

-

To have known
To have been
To have loved

-

A tragic remembrance of the glory days
Yet a comfort
Knowing that the life that has been lived was better
Than one that has only known the fierce curse of
Fear and anger

-

As the winds blow the petals of life away
It all was just another thing
That has come and gone

The simplicity of it all
I find rather frustrating
It is truly so hard, yet so easy
To understand

Yet we spend every moment of our waking day
Trying to figure it out

Why?
Why is living so hard to understand

ASHES OF A WORLD

The ashes of the weight of the world
As it crashes down on the heroes
Of today

The world is in blazes
As the toxicity
Of the evil and harshness

The pieces of the light is fading
Through the heaven
Is still growing

CURSE OF THE CRIMSON EMPIRE

As I look back on my life
all the struggles and sorrows
all the things I wish I could take back
all the things I should have said
I wish I could change the past
but it can't be

FORGOTTEN EMPIRE

I'm a soldier of a falling empire
One that the world used to love
Now it is nothing but
a faded memory

VERNAL

The blue sky
The evening breeze
A sense of happiness
Washes over me

Clouds float in
Such a majestic way
Who but a fool
Would not stop
And stare

The trees sway
The birds chirp
The sound of the creek
Is enough to calm
Ones heart

The way the setting
Sun paints a
Sea of wondrous light
And casts a shadow
Over the snow covered
Mountain

All these things
Give me what
Every man craves for
The pure feeling
Of peace

A WHITE DOVE IN THE MIDST OF THE STORM

The Truth
Why does it hurt
Is it because we are
too scared to face it
Or because we never
knew it
Or
because we knew it
We just didn't want to
believe it…

VOW

I will make a vow
To you
A vow saying
I will never let you fall
I will never leave your side
Through your darkest nights
Through your darkest fears
I promise to fight
for you
That is my vow

DESOLATE WINTER

We meet standing on
A familiar road
For the final time

A broken hello
A sorrowful goodbye
Then we walk past one another
Away from the memories
Of the days we shared

Love I thought
Would last
Has finally run
Its course

This house that was filled
With joy
Is my desolate
Prison

You turn around
Watching as I grow smaller
A final kiss of the sun
Before it leaves the day

Can this tragedy
Ever reach its final act
I can remember the smiles

Remember the laughs
All the things
I wish I could forget

This world I know
Is falling apart
What will I do without you
It was your choice
Your action
But now I have to rebuild
What is left of me
Do I have enough
Love to

It hurts so bad
When I think of it
But I let you go
Walk away
The only way I
Will be able to heal

DARKNESS

Darkness
Its vines with thorns
Circling you
Piercing your skin
As the weight of your sins
Crushes you from within

A numb feeling
That never disappears
No matter how much you try to fill it
With the warmth of love and family

It's being in an endless hell
The day that memories haunt you

At night thoughts keep you awake
Not wanting to sleep
Because you known when you wake
The light that let you
See in the dark
Is gone

THE WATCHER

The clouds sit low in the sky
As the fog creeps into the bay
The moon hidden from the shore
A view that no longer exists

Cold air rushes by as
I wander along the tide covered beach
Lost in a graveyard of ghosts

I try and find my way to safety
Blind in every direction
Until I hear a voice calling out to guide me
A quiet gentle voice
One that drips of honey and pure ecstasy
A voice that lures me towards the end
Of the almost non existent shore

As I follow the siren's song
I go deeper and deeper into the water
Cold piercing shards
Steal my very being
However, I continue until I feel my feet
Give way underneath
And as if by choice
I do no attempt to stay
Above the surface

Water begins to fill my lungs
As I sink further and further
Into my watery grave

As my breath stills
My eyes look up one last time
My life flashing before my eyes

I am but a lost soul
Looking for my final resting place
Somewhere between the night and
The watery grave
I now call home

BREAKING THE HORIZON

As the days pass by
I'm becoming a foreigner to your warmth
Fearing one day
I may forget what it feels like to be in the
Warmth of the sun

To say I miss you
Is an understatement
I want no happiness
Because you were it
The sun that helped me bloom

Now I live in the dark
My soul withering away
A life without my sun

CRUELTY

I look for you
Only to be disappointed
Reminded of the crippling truth
I tried so hard to bury inside
Do anything not to feel
To not face this world
This cruel world that took you from
Me

POLLUTION

Oil seeps through the cracks
Veins travel into the water
Intoxicating the pure gift of the heavens
Polluting the valleys below

The poison spreads like wildfire
Consuming more and more

The spark that ignited the embers
Is tragic nonetheless
For it wanted to grow
But was dimmed within

As tears fall from the crying sky
The flames of desire slowly die
But a trickle of oil
That seeped through hell
Made its way to a single flame
And as if meant to be
It would cause a reaction
Nobody would have wanted to see

GUIDANCE

I plead to those who came before me
For guidance
Guidance for the journey that lies before me
One that is unknown to me
Hoping when I meet her
I may find comfort
The type I've been waiting for

PROMISE MADE

A silent promise kept
Realization to protect it at all costs
Love never shown but runs deep beneath the skin
Tears shed as a smile breathes through the horror that overwhelms us
A promise made and kept
So that one day
You will be happy

NATURE

The soft hue of golden brown
Shining through the design of trees
That call the hidden valley in the mountains
Their sanctuary

The glow
Projecting onto the mossy ground below
The rays illuminating moths
As they fly around
In their hypnotizing dance

The creatures grazing
Upon the vegetation
Giving life to those
All around

The quietness of the forest
The lack of society
Only the gentle whispers of the wildlife

This hidden paradise
This piece of heaven
Blessed by God

A gift to mankind,
A beautiful thing to take
A man's breath away
The endless gravel road

I find myself walking
Is as empty as a distant memory
A skeleton to what once was

FORETOLD

Foretold
That we all will walk the shores
Beyond the horizon

That the hands that formed us out of clay
Will be the ones that reach out to us
When it is our time
To return to dust

That the stars that surround us
In our skies
Eventually fade into the
Midnight sun

A parallel to the fate of all man
That the energy that was formed and shaped
Into a masterpiece
Will one day dissolve and shatter
To one day return to the universe
And possibly be reborn

And as the clock that stood untouched
By man, finally turns to stone
The waves of the seas calm
The winds that bring forth peace and destruction
Cease to be

The dawn will plead with the night
But she will not reveal her fortunes told
For she has said that

Even if all the skies go dark
And the waters dry up
And the land burns

The birds will still sing
And life will go on

For the story of the present is written
By those who've seen the past
And wish to build
A better land
From which the children
Can prosper from

WALK WITH THE DEVIL

I walk in the devil's heart
Demons and horrors appear and disappear
As if toying with me
Waiting to see if I'd run in fear
Or continue forward in defiance

The sun burns my skin
Rocks pierce the soles of my feet
Lips cracked and my throat is dry
My vision sitting between hallucination and reality

Weariness tears at me and I wonder why i continue
Down this path
Why not collapse
Let my knees hit the ground
And let myself crumble
And wither away with time

For reasons I do not understand
I choose to wander
Even through the valley of death
For I am not ready to shake
The hands of the devil

THERE IS NO SUNLIGHT
IN PURGATORY

If the rain is suppose to
Wash the blood away
Why is my soul
Still stained

Guilty seeing the sunrise
Guilty living without you
Guilty knowing it's easier
Now that you've left

To weep
Seems beyond ironic
As if Caesar tripped
And fell on his own sword
Feels like betrayal
As if I'm being drowned
In silver coins

Cruelly hating the warmth
Because I have forced
Myself to be entombed
In this wintery mirage
It would seem
It's easier
To roll over and hide
Then face the blessing
Of a new day

There is no comfort in the past
A fool trying to stay somewhere
That has come and gone
Yet like a twist of fate
It is the only place
That feels
Like home

Thankful for life
However
It feels I'm growing weaker inside
Yes
I know you must look
At the better things
Have faith that the heavens
May weep
And blessings rain down
Galactic aura to surround us
Brightening the world
Around you

Now it's gone
Shackled to the ruins
Insanity is now
The only place I know

Remembering you
Only brings a tearing feeling
Of love and sadness
I dont hate you
How could I
I know it was the right thing

Just like the stars in the
Majestic galaxy above
Sometimes
People shine brighter
Out from behind the shadows

Remembering your face
Reminds me of the pain
Mental collapse of my
Fragile tormented soul
Drives me to the point
Past insanity

Tell me why
Why did you leave
That's all I want to know
All I want to understand
You were so much more
Than a moment
In time

The guilt eats at me
I'm slowly killing myself
The constant guilt
The bloody regret
It's as though I'm stabbing a knife
Straight into my back

Seems like the waters
That flowed through the valley
To the hidden meadows
To give life to the
Thousands of wildflowers
Has died

No more than a
Graveyard of memories
Memories of the time I
Feel like I tricked you
into having hope

I cant imagine
Leaving the warmth of the sun
I know it's the way
The fruit falls off the tree
And the sun rays cascade from
The majestic fields and silent hills

That one day
We all
Have to walk
On our own

To leave the embrace
Of an angel
That smiled as she left

Realizing as I stand
In the battlefield
Of my own minds invention
Maybe hell isn't so bad
Because
There is no sunlight in purgatory

LIGHT BY THE SEA

The symbol that
Stood before the city
The city that welcomed all
A city that stood firm along the coast
Where the sea bled into the land

Named after a king, named after a conqueror
A city known as the Bride Of Mediterranean
A place where people from around the world
Could come and bask in the wonders of the world

A ray of light needed to be seen
For the ships in the dark
Had no star to guide them
To the safety of the docks

A symbol that was built
Created to be a guide
A beacon of hope
The sailors could trust
To find the safety of the
City of culture
The city known as
The Bride of the Mediterranean

COLLAPSE OF THE KINGDOM

One could let the walls of his fortress fall
So that the enemy can rush in
Stealing, destroying, corrupting
Everything in sight

Locking themselves in the tower,
The coward awaits its final moments
Where the walls will collapse
Taking them away

As the sound of rushing feet, clashing metal,
The sound of a sword cutting through the air
A sound that thunders at the door
Shaking the ground
As if it was God's fury

A final breath is drawn
And as it grows dark
The eyes of the innocent
Are shown a light from above
Giving a chance of comfort and peace

Where the thoughts of man no longer matter
And the hypocrisy no longer dictates who you are

FROM WITHIN

A dark tunnel
Filled with smoke
Remembrance of the past
Hollowed inside

An illusion
The eyes pierce the deception
The warm aura is there
Flourishing in its light
Yet it's been forsaken

Forced into an open cell
If chosen it could heal the
Garden that is wilting

But it just sits there and waits
Except for the few times it sees the dawn

It's open
So why doesn't it leave
Why does the haunting
Feeling consume

Blindness caused by cruelty
The sweet cruelty of life
The chilling desire for warmth

Is sunk too deep for one to reach
Unless it is time for the seed
To grow

Waiting to find the sign
The God given gift of hope
To which they so crave
Only to find no clue
To lead them

Who do you curse
The one who gave you life
The one who is selfish
Do you scream at the one
Who was suppose to comfort you
Or does one blame themselves
For not finding the will
To try

At this crossroad
They know this is the final opportunity
Been on paradise for far too long
Only to realize it was a desert waste land

Hoping to find the thing
To save their last bit of life
From their mummified soul

Confusion sets in
And they begin to believe it is impossible
That they should let their very being
Fade away

To be forgotten
A piece of history
A memory of long ago

-

To find the source
Of their misfortune
And untimely tragedy
Whatever causes the sky to turn gray
And the seas to roar and cry
As it claims another life

Wish to understand their own destruction
To burn Rome and rebuild
An even stronger empire
One without the fear of betrayal,
Failure, loss, and regret

-

The fear is the cause of misunderstanding
A stone in the path of moving forward
The haunting thoughts, memories,
One worked so hard to bury it all
In the deepest pits of their mind

CHAINS

A seagull flying over the vast open sea
That shines under the heavenly sun
Will only ever view it
As a majestic masterpiece
Filled with the promise of fuel for their day

They dare not understand
The way a sailor
Views it as he
Races around the boat

The crew trying to secure the sails
As a hurricane,
Like the voice of hell,
Rages on

Waves towering over them
Like a mountain towers over the humble mouse
The fear that grips the heart of man

THE WALLS OF TROY

A fatal mistake
A victorious triumph
A mistake of judgment
Aphrodite would tell

The greed of man
A misfortune in beauty
As the sounds of war
Are heard all around the world

The skies dim
As the fleet heads to
The shore of the heavenly walls
Apollo watching over his city
As his enemies come

No man could say
Who would stand among the Gods
Or be lost to the sandy shore

Nor if victory was rescue
Or destruction of the enemy
No one could have foretold
The fatal mistake
The legendary duel,
An unfortunate weakness

And as the smoke
Began to rise
And the gods stirred in their seats
The battle of legacies
Began

Warriors from both fronts
Would meet among
The valley of ghosts
A sacrifice to win and protect

As the soles of his sandals
Touch the earth
He knew
He would never be allowed to
Return home again

FREE

Free
I must be free
For if I am not free
I shall be similar to that
Of a wingless bird
That forever must watch the sky
Wishing to fly
Or
A tree that may
Never know
What lies beyond its vast
Sea of mountains

If I was to choose
Oh, but one sky to see
One silhouette
For all eternity

Nebuchadnezzar
Would be whom
I'm mimicking
Chained to the podium
For all eyes to see

Alexander held no reigns
To what the world
Offered
For he went out and conquered

Beyond the horizon
His heart knew no tame

Breath must know
The chill of the mountain air
Cheeks must feel
The breeze of an
Autumn day
Skin must warm
Like a summer tea

Sail across the ocean
Columbus looking for a
New destination
Fly high in the sky
To overlook the world
And bask in glory
See the greens that are
Vibrant and show the luscious
Plant life

The blue of the sea
That holds more secrets
Than man would ever believe

Let go and let your conscious guide you
Beyond the stars
Beyond the earth

As long as my will carries me
These binds will never hold me
Forever,
I will be free

AFTER DARK

I wish on a star
A wish to bring back
That smile that caused
The spring to come and go

Now, everytime I think of you
The night begins to fall
Maybe seeing you
Would clear this
Sunless night

I hate that time
Hasn't softened these wounds
That consume my fragile heart
How many tear stained faces
And sleepless nights must
I embrace until I'm fine

Does it seem like I have grown colder
A foreigner to the warmth
Of the summer sun
Look up and the moon has risen
Yet everything stands still

As the wind takes away
These autumn leaves
Can it take away the
Emptiness you caused me

Time flies by
The seasons change
Will this pain
Ever go away

Will this be our final goodbye
Or an excuse for peace tonight

Wish our memories would fade away
Leave this world, a shooting star
Wish I could turn back time
Maybe I could save you

If I had said
Those words to you then
Would night have come
Would this cruel darkness have
Consumed you

Honestly I hate seeing you
In my dreams
Cause your face haunts me everytime
A good moment comes my way

Childlike it is,
I wish our paths never crossed
Wished the memories would fade
Like smoke in the rain.

I hate the fact that
I can never be happy because
Of the pain and regret
You cause me

I want to shut you out
Cast you aside
Try anything
To make it hurt less
I try to erase you
Like the mistake on this paper
But selfishly I can't
Because it was you
Who was in pain

The blossoms don't seem
To bloom like before
The spring will never be the same
If I could reverse time
I would give you my hand
Too bad I can't make amends

Maybe one day
We'll meet at the crossroads
And smile like we used to
Until that day
I wish you were here

Another season has come and gone
The moon has gone down
Time is slowly moving
Maybe it is you forgiving me
Hopefully this cold season, an endless winter
Will end
So I can live in peace
Finally be at peace.

ONE STEP BACK

These walls I have
built are crumbling down
Can you hear
my heart cry
As I slip into
the darkness

STAND TALL LIKE A GIANT

The strongest people
are the ones
that have been to hell and back
and still believe
there is good
in this world

WHO WE ARE

These are the times where we get lost.
Some people say we are not ourselves
and when we ask them how, they give us
some random reason.
Sometimes those reasons are so vague
We don't know whether they are true or not.

Things happen in our lives that change us.
We grow out of things and into new things.
Who are we to say, this is not the real us?

Maybe because we spend part of our lives
with our parents.
We pick up on their thoughts, their opinions, their actions.
So maybe the change is good.
Maybe it helps decide who we are and who we are not

LIVE AND LET GO

If things aren't meant to be
don't cry
Move on

There is no use
crying over somethings
When you can work on something
that is greater than you can imagine

GRAVE

The agony I feel
When the words
I spoke to you
Continue to haunt me,
Is beyond measure

Through words spoken
In anger
Are meant to be harmful
Neglected
They still cause more damage
And are harder to forgive

I say them out of frustration
Cause I see you
And I feel inferior
As if we do the same thing
But you get the praise
While I feel forgotten

Jealous for how you have grown

I speak words of anger
And you do the same
But this dance can only
Last so long

I fear it is too late
To heal the wounds
We've caused

You will walk away
And forget me

Yes,
The agony haunts me
As if I'm being buried alive
In my own grave

PART 2:

Antiqui colant
antiquum dierum
"Let the ancients worship
the ancient of days"

THE JUDGE

Who are we to Judge
    If we do not know
    the full picture
If you have never walked
    a thousand miles in their shoes
    don't look at them with your gavel
We do not know where people
    have been
    or
    what they are going through
    can't we all agree that we
Are all human
    that no one is better than
    one another
Why can't we just love
    and be kind to all
Why Judge?
    It doesn't make you a
    better person
    It makes you look
    small
Judge not
    No matter what people say
    No one is perfect
    We are not meant to be

MANKIND

I often wonder why mankind acts the way it does.
    When we have hit rock bottom or met the hand of death
    or even shaken hands with the Devil,
    we see our true self.
Our mistakes and sins, we see what is truly important
    and what is not.

We live in a repetitive cycle, never seeing our inner demons.
    So many people live their lives, never giving a thought about
        their actions
    never thinking about what they do to others.
They live a good life, full of lies and deception.

So few of us can break free from this
    deadly cycle.
Live our lives truthfully.
    Yet some of us are stuck in the middle.
    Not knowing which way or whom to trust

PRESSURE FROM WITHIN

It is impossible to say
Words cannot describe
What it takes
To feel alright

Lessons come
Lessons learned
Yet the child within
Still falters

A change of scenery
Shifts focus
A million stars fall
Only a handful are born

Pressure rises
Seeping from beneath the ground
Only a frail flower
To keep it calm

-

Waves crash against the coast
One by one
The edges fall

The ice that cracked
From so long agony
Has ironically healed
By the shadowed sin
The prophet hidden away
Having been cursed
For the problems at bay

He only sits and ponders
Life and death
Only for a song to be whispered
And be shattered by the wind

The skies break as the angels sing
The sun emerging for a new day

The will that was shackled by ones
False greed, regret, expectancies
Sorrows deed

It rusts under the healers feet
As they take the hands
And lead them to be free

-

Remembrance is not a curse
A blessing of hope, love, and pain
For without pain
You can never know love
Without love
You can never know pain

-

Bitter words
Tear at the heart
Blind with rage
Tears the family apart

The bridge crumbles under the weight
Waters may run
Overflowing with the
Fierce sense of grace
Threatens to drown,
Threatening to save

Rest assured they mean you no harm
As they only wish to purify
The weight of your soul

GREY WOLF HUNTS
THE BLACK LAMB

Never let the memories
of the people
who hurt you
take over
they have no power
over how you
choose to live
your life

WE WALK AND FADE AWAY

Never tried to see the way you look at me
now do you despise me
hate the thought of me
I'm so sorry
now all that's left are
these bittersweet tears
the distant look in your eyes

RAIN

The raindrops fall against the window
as the darkened sky sends thunderous echos
to shatter this silence
that has grown in my life

DEATH AT THE
HANDS OF FATE

Life is beautiful
No matter how you look at it
It's beautiful
Through joy
You see its true beauty
Some would say
"How can you see beauty
In so much hate and tragedy?"

To which I say

"Those are the moments
Where we see people come together and see their compassion"
In those moments
You see the purest of love

OF LIFE

Choices are annoying
You contemplate on what you should do
And once you make a decision and go with it
You often wonder if it was
The right choice

Even down the road
At the very end of the road

You'll look back and question
Your life choices

MEANINGLESS WORDS

They say it gets easier
But I believe that to be a lie
It gets harder as time
Passes by

Truly I do not believe
I will truly even accept it
I don't know
That I will truly ever
Believe it
Naturally I believe
It becomes a part of us
Not something we learn to live with
But learn to adjust around

No I will most likely never be
The same or okay again
Frankly I do not
Know if I want to be okay
Because how is life okay
Without you
It's just another day
With a little less warmth
Though I try and stand under
The sun more
No it's a tragic fact of life
Something all fear
But secretly crave
That hillside with the kind
scenery

BROKEN BONES

If we condemn and fight evil
Why is it we hate the truth
Why do we choose to ignore the truth

If we want a just world
A world that prospers
Why are we accepting a society built on
Broken bones

FEAR

Fear drives a man insane
Whether it be madness or power
It simply does not go away

DAY BY DAY

Days they go by like dead leaves
Crossing the road by the forgotten wind
Like sand that is blown away,
Finding rest in an unknown place

Like film that unwinds
Toppling over the time it took
To put it in order

The days seem to just come and go
Becoming a blurry vision
As if the world was just a repeat

MISSING YOU

I miss you
I am afraid I'll forget you
Live day by day
With you only as a memory
That I Remember
Every now and then
Or when I need an excuse
To explain my anger
Or sadness

I do not want to accept it
The fate that I could not
Change because
You were always there

SHATTERED HOURGLASS

The sands of time
Flood the hourglass
Trickling down
Reflecting the sun's rays

A call of remembrance
As the light of day hits
The mountain range;
Painting a portrait of life

The retelling of a beautiful story
Obese whose pages,
Whose chapters
Will forever be remembered

MALIGNANCY

It sits and waits for you to fall into a deep slumber
As your breath steadies and your mind drifts off
Into your timeless dreams

It watches silently, like a hunter watches its prey
Eyes filled with the desire to defeat you
To strip away all your hope

Slowly with precise movements
It gets closer
Long thin legs,
Black almost mist like
With an eerie aura
It makes its way towards you

Lanky hands with talons as sharp as knives
Wait to grab you when it can

As it places its hands on your head
It watches every move you have ever made
It wickedly smiles and laughs like a weeping banshee
Finally it invades your defenseless body
To try and take over
Oh how I wish it wasn't so
For this is no man

No demon we have dreamed about
No it's something worse
Something that can cripple
The strongest man and anger the kindest mother
It can give and take away
No my friend it is not something of legend
It is a cruel thing

SWEET CORRUPTION

Darkness
Darkness all around
Even after I close my eyes
There is a darkness deep within

Not that of evil
Nor the absence of light

It is an abyss
That surrounds the mind
A comforting warmth
That draws you in
And asks that you never leave

TRUE

Forgiveness is one of those things that
Takes a lot of energy to do
But once you have accepted it
The weight of the world collapse
And you are truly free
Like a puzzle missing only one piece
The shattered pieces of a priceless vase

There are pieces that won't go back together
No matter how hard you try

Flying through the air
In a wave of confusion
My maze of memories is crumbling around me

THE WAKE OF MAN

The glowing emerald water
Fades into the sea of baby blue
Golden halo that stands above the world
Giving life to the creatures below
The breath of life that was given
To the man
Who would become the father of people

A treasure that is so easily lost
And forgotten throughout the voyage
Of time

Tales are passed down
Through the generations
Until one day
They are forgotten
Like dust in the wind
And waves in the ocean

And as the crimson fades
The sound of the harps
Is heard as the sun
Bleeds Into the night
Time never seems to unravel or unlock
The foundations of the mystery

It holds no feelings
No emotions
Unlike that of life

Time will go on
Long after you and I
Are long gone

SECOND IN TIME

Is this all life is
When we die
Our loved ones
Settle our affairs
Pack our things away
And preserve the concept of us

Reorganize the house
And life goes on
Is that all we are
Just a second in time

THE BEAUTIFUL TRAGEDY

Life is a beautiful tragedy
We live to die
Die to live
Yet never truly live

Slaving away just to try and survive
We waste our lives
Never really knowing
The taste of life

We just work until we choose to stop
Wasting away our final years
Until death takes us

FABRICATION

Forgiveness is not fabricated
So the sins and faults of others
Suddenly vanish

It is simply a healing
For your own soul
A chance to renew
This version of yourself

TRAGEDY

Tragedy is one of those bittersweet moments in life
You remember all the good and all the bad times
But is also shows you peoples true nature

If one lets go of the pain
To cherish the joy and grow
And humble themselves
Then they can be happy

But if one holds on and indulges in the frustrations
And instead of creating a stronger bond
With those around them
They push them away

Created unwanted tension
A tension that pulls on the bonds that hold everyone together
Until one day
It eventually snaps

UNDER THE RED SEA

Lying under the stars
On a lake of red
Diamonds fill my eyes
As I gasp for air
That only thing that keeps me alive

Blind to the truth
Indulged in the lies
Wanting me to accept tyranny
When I scream for liberty

The alienation of those
Who walk in the path of
Disenchantment
Cripples the foundations of the Pantheon
Our ancestors fought
To protect

VISION

It's a rainbow after the storm
The sun rising from the dark
In a frightening way
A voice calls out to comfort
Those who wait in fright
In fear of judgment;
Silent crying can be heard
As the terrors of the darkness
Finally begin to plague the Earth
The devil grinning ear to ear

Pastures of happiness
Or dungeons of peace
A hazy view or a beautiful vision

The scales tip from one side to the next
The heart is a heavy burden
For those who are innocent and those
Who believe they are

Simplicity has confused man
Therefore unable to see the beauty of it all
He lies only in the corrupt, unjust,
Lies of himself
What a sad destruction to mankind

BALLAD OF A FOOL

I stood before God and spoke words that
Were never meant to be believed
The man that betrayed the lamb
Was given a pardon

A pardon that was an excuse
For the belief that everyone sins

Betrayal on both ends
The hidden desire to forget
To hide it
To sweep it under the rug
So the fires can multiply
And burn down everything

Instead of blaming the criminal
The victim blames themselves
Blame themselves for something
They have no control over
Guilt ridden over the betrayal
The mistake of one person
Killed the garden
The place of peace of paradise
Beginning with the rose

Now the gardener feeds
The garden every now and then
For the beauty of the petals

The aroma of the flowers
Remain in their daydreams

Truly impossible to find
The cause of said tragedy
But its true it began with the guilt
That was born when one stabbed themselves
With a guilt ridden sword
A guilt that was wrongly nurtured over time

WHAT IT IS I FEAR

I have become the very thing I feared the most
The one thing I said I'd never be
I have let my anger, my failures
Get the best of me

Instead of being the love
I so cherished and longed for
I have become the hate
I wished to fight and overcome

I can feel its gripped, its arms surrounding me
Trapping me in an nonexistent prison
An illusion I created
One I have used to justify my every action,
Every thought, every word I have ever spoken

I close my eyes because I do not want to accept
What I have already accepted
That this is what I have become
I am nothing more than a failure
To myself
The thing I have always hated

ANUBIS

I often wonder
if people think
there are no
consequences for their
actions
and if they are fine
living like that

WHO WE ARE

The parting of ways
Whether it be
Only for a moment
Or forever

It quenches the heart
Forcing it to thinking
To yearn for something
It can never find nor ever have

Oh, the ache that comes
With a yearning soul

MAIDEN OF THE EARTH

Unjust is the maiden
For the ground shall be stirred;
Seas will dry and the mountains flattened
Yet she will stand tall
In all her glory

The fear of judgment
Not crossing her mind
As she looks down at the world
With a grin on her face
The sins of man
Stripping away from her flesh

Her naked form
Stands before everyone
Its beauty becoming one
With the land as the blood
From her veins
Seeps through the crack of the earth

Seeping into the skin of the beast
The creature that has been resting
For the past thousand years
Begins to stir
The earth awaiting its final moments

With a final breath,
The maiden ceases to be

Her once life filled body
Becoming the dust of the past
The last glimpse of the dawn
Before a storm

Breaking through the ashes
Of the fires
That surround the land
That once protected this fair maiden;
The creature embodies the smoke
That fills the air

It hunts for the
Origin of species-
The one who created all

The temptation to devour
The heart of the universe
Is ever so pleasing
So morally corrupting
That it cannot handle the temptation

Reeking of the sins of man
Eyes rotting away from the tortures
And the deception of the devil
Skin burning and melting away
From its bones
As a punishment from
The almighty

It screams in pure agony
When it discovers that the
Temptress of its dream
The demon of the night;
Had been laid to rest
Eons ago- only to come forth

Every few hundred years-
To be reborn and to go about the world
Observing and testing
The souls of mankind
Weighing the hearts
To see if they shall be blessed
Or cursed, once again

The screams of this creature
Are heard throughout the world
Only for them to be silenced
Cut short by its own consumption
The hatred and pure deception it had
For the world and all those who inhabit it
Fueled the fire
That eventually consumed its being

Exploding in a massive ball
Of bloodied and cursed ash
A wave of burning wind
Rushing through the brush and the
Trees
Races and encircles the ashes
Creating a whirlwind before
Sucking it down through the cracks
Of the land that the maiden
Had created

-

Unjust is the maiden
For the ground shall be stirred;
Seas will dry and the mountains flattened
Yet she will stand tall
In all her glory

The maiden stands alone
in all her grace
Her blood blending in with
The rivers that flow
Through the land

The crimson
Replenishing the soul
That created the earth
And the land that once
Reigned with terror and agony
Has once again been blessed
By she who shall remains nameless

The skies becoming clearer
As the smoke and ash fade
The moon consuming the skies
That will one again
Give birth to the light
Of the world
And the creations
That sustain the very ones
Who inhabit it

May the land be blessed
By the very soul of it
The one that fights for it
The one who nurtures
The one who is apart of it
And continues to be the mother
Of all

THE TRAGEDY OF
THE INNOCENT

The sins of man,
Are often overlooked
By the eyes court
For money, power, and greed
Can hide anything

Yet for the poor,
whose sins are often less drastic
And cruel, than that
Of the wealthy and powerful
Are thrown to the lions
To be devoured and silenced-
Their sins are proclaimed throughout
The land
Meant to be worn as a badge
Of shame and disappointment

Self proclaimed justice
Is brought to their feet;
Punishment waiting for them
As if they have waiting for this moment
Since before they were born
Where the wicked drink the blood
Of the innocent,

Never fearing, never knowing
The sheer terror,
the pure taste of judgment

For who are they to be judge,
Who are they to fear punishment
For they are the ones who write the laws
And use the laws to their advantage

One good deed of theirs must be enough
To justify and disguise all the corruption
They commit in the shadows

-

Gilded do they live
Feeding the tree gold and blood-
Never seeing that it already had died
And has been rotting away for centuries

When the poor come to them
Pleading for justice,
Praying for help,
Crying for the truth

They simply toss them a bone
Believing that the leftovers of their
Decisions and livelihood
Will be enough to satisfy
And quench the thirst
So that the voices of the majority
Will grow silent

-

The night has taken over the day
For far too long
The streets grow in shame
Filling with filth, disease
A place unfit for living
A cruel reality for those
Making an effort to survive

-

The few that live in euphoria
Wining and dining on all the
Luxuries provided by the devil
The indulgence corrupting what
Little is left of their soul
Chaining their fate
One they shall not escape
When the day of judgment comes;

Hiding, waiting for the moment
The dream is shattered-
Waiting for the one who will
Take that fall

-

Born and raised
In glorified love and fashion
With the blessings of the land
Within his grasp
Hidden away in the safety of
The garden
Never allowed to see the weeds
That surround the outside

He stands alone on the
Steps leading up to the pearly gates
Growing and learning
Doing what was believed to be right
Never knowing that
The wine was spilling over

Never knowing that
He was becoming
the lamb to be slaughtered

In the way the Book of Life
Reads the names of those
Who shall be saved

The names of the fallen
Were spoken and the memories
And emotions of the pain
That has been building up
For the past century
Have finally begun to stir
The vengeance overflows
In the goblet of life
And the fires begin to emerge
All over the the City of Lights

A reign of terror began
And as the sun lights up the day
The fires and the voices of the masses
Brighten the night
As the devil stands above the city
With a wicked grin about his face

Watching and waiting for the blood
Of the innocent to once again
Be spilt

And fall upon the land
So that the Whore of Babylon
May get a moment of satisfaction

-

Years going by
The flames of anger and frustration
Growing more and more
Waiting to consume the garden

The man has grown up
Becoming a symbol of a nation
The hope for the people

To marry a bride of innocence and beauty
Is one of the only gifts
God has ever granted him
For he foresaw the curse that would
Later take the man

-

Who knew that within a few years
He would be hiding
Forsaken by the people who he
So wished to protect-
Cursed by the children
For the crimes of the elders
Of generations past

Looking over to his family,
The precious sweet gift
That would be ripped from
His grasp
Ceasing to be one by one;

Knowing that he would not
Be able to protect them
Feeling as if he failed being
The husband and father
They needed
A cruel and unjust gavel was struck down
The weight and sins of the wicked
Strip the angel of its wings
The principalities of darkness
Laughing as the dance around with them
Mocking him as he is chained
And thrown away
Like a dog that has served its purpose
And is waiting to be put
Out of its misery

-

A man who is no stranger to blood
And death-
A man who is judged and disregarded
As human
By the people who relish
In the art he so hates

He fears no judgment of man
Nor fears the judgment of God
For he knows that the deeds he does
Go hand in hand with the work
Of the Lord's word

The darkness that brings forth
The light that the people
Have been yearning for;
The feared angel
That awaits the day

The unjust blessings and
Cries of gratitude are quieted

That the promise of peace
The pastures of paradise
The hymns of the angels
May ease his heart
And that he may
Be able to make amends
With those whom he has
Devoured

So that his mind and soul
May be at ease
When he meets the king
Of kings

The cold foggy morning
Hiding the tears of those who
Love him so
A blessing in disguise
For the one whose fate
Will be handed to him
Coating him in a veil
That hides him from
The demons whom hope to steal
His soul

The ground uneven
The air crisp and the smell of death
Weighs heavy as the servants
That once served him,
Now serve those who
Stand hand in hand with Judas

The silver coins in their hands
Weighing nothing for their corrupt
Conscious is clear

Closer and closer they get
Hymns of the angels-
That pray for his salvation- can scarcely
Be heard over the shout and cries
Of the people
Who will bring forth a new dawn
To their beloved country

He closes his eyes and shuts out the sounds
Of his beloved people
The very ones who will wear his blood
As a right to their revolution

His heart races in fear and sadness
For he knows it is not them
Who has brought this upon him
But those he thought he could trust
Shaking he lets out the breath
He never knew he was holding
Slowly breathing in and out in hopes
He may steady his heart
For he knows his time is short
And that he will never see his family again

The coach stops cold in its track
The jolt tossing him forward-
As he reaches out to steady himself
The doors are thrown open and he
Breathes out one more time
Collecting his thoughts and

Emotions, he steps out–
Showing no fear, no worry

With grace, dignity, and power
He walks among the crowd
That screams rants at him,
Throwing anything at him in order
To destroy and ruin his pride
Trying to humiliate him
In every way possible

The cold breeze nips at the nape
Of his neck,
The beautiful locks of hair
Stripped and shortened
So that nothing will stop
The verdict that was given to him

-

The crowd begins to quiet as the man
Steps upon the platform
The colors that represent life and death
Moving in the breeze

Glancing down
He watches as his next victim
Weaves through the crowd
The weight of his soul
Crashing down again

-

The innocent man
Upon hearing the crowd
Begin to whisper

Raises his head higher than
He had held it
And as if he had been pierced
By an arrow that was shoot
True by Paris himself-
He was shot with a sense
Of tranquility

As if hypnotized by the man
That stood before him
A vision of light illuminating
The aura around him
Dark wings reaching out around him
Encircling the man
Whose face
Whose presence
The very man
Who was the Grim Reaper,
Himself

-

His feet move on their own
His very soul the only thing
That is allowing him to move forward

In that moment
The eyes of Death and Life met
Death reaching out and life taking it
Allowing him to lead him
To the pearly gates
The podium that was laid before
The valley of death
For all eyes to see

Where the dead, the living
The Devil and God
Could watch this
Once in a lifetime event
A never before seen performance
An act that would send shivers
Down the spines of all
Who stood in power and greed

A man who is feared by all
A man who is cursed by all
A man who is innocent of sin-
But must commit one of the most
Barbaric of them all for justice

A man who is guilty of living
Taking the burden of the wickedness
Of others
The lamb that was brought to slaughter
The first time in the history of
This fair nation

As his conscious came back to him
He stood before the people
And instead of the shouts
Instead of the weak and weary
The thin and poor

Stood the people
In a field of pure gold,
The breeze swaying the white robes
All wore
In that moment he understood

Understood that fact that
Everything that was happening
Was not something of hate
Or of disrespect
It was fear
All men are born equal but
It is the few that corrupt the scales
Of the world
And force the people
To fight to stay alive

Everyone believes in living
And everyone has the right
To find pure joy and happiness
The masses held no hatred to him
But to the idea that
Being born was a curse and not a blessing

We are all children of the creator
We all belong in paradise
For that he could hold no grudge
No hatred towards these people
These people who were simply tired
Of being seen as nothing but scum

-

And as the man was led
Up the stairs
Across the bone covered graveyard
That held the gallows-
To lay down
On the wooden bed
Of the device that would take
Hundreds of lives after his

His heart calmed
The air stilled, the sun not threatening
To emerge and give life
To this tragic affair

And the prays of the angels
Became music to his ears
He would fear nothing
In this crowning moment

I shall fear no evil
Is what the reaper spoke
As he watch the crowd hold their breath
Meeting the eyes of the devil
Once again, he closed his eyes
And with the release of his grasp
The blade finally pierces his neck

Like Icarus, Who wanted nothing more
Than to reach the heights no man Had yet reached,
The man fell short of that dream-
He was taken from this Earth
Far sooner than he should have been
Forever doomed to be remembered
By His dying moment

And as the Reaper raises the Kings head
Above the crowd
Instead of tears and sorrow
Weeping and cries of injustice
His blood is welcomed with cheers and laughter
A standing ovation that defined a revolution

RIGHTEOUS GLORY

Another tear stained face
another broken heart
if this is a story
where's the hero
in all his righteous glory

REGRETS

Please don't cry to me
Cause I don't want
To listen
To all your foolish sins

You were the one
Who played the cards
That were dealt to you
Trusting in your choice
Committing to your decision

Should I shut your eyes
And hide the pain
You caused inside

Though you see the pain
You've caused
You do not believe that
You owe an apology
Or the fact that one
Will not be enough
To right the wrongs
You can't rewrite what
You have done
The past is in the past
There is no changing that

however,
It can still haunt you

-

Should have thought about
The devil's kiss
Before you let yourself
Get seduced
Those silver coins
Only pay for your final fate

FALLING FROM GRACE

Don't know how this could happen
Never understand the way
this life works
Why can't it be a dream
a nightmare that will go away

If I don't forgive
I'll fall from grace
but if I do
I will still fall
So let me fall
engulfed in my own
demise

PART 3:

Ab aeterno:
"From the Eternal"

WALKING INTO THE MOONLIGHT

People say they wish
They could turn back time
But I have to ask
Why?

Why relive the moments you cherish so much
Why revisit the nightmares that haunt you so much
Why experience the hurt you have felt already

To those people I say
How selfish can you be
Is the present too terrible for you to except

If looking back
And reliving memories
Is all you want in your life
You will only ever see the past
Never looking or striving
For a cherished future
One that you could have created
If you didn't relive the past

ANGEL WINGS

What will happen, when it all comes to an end
Will I fall to hell or fly on angel wings
Angel wings to take me to you,
so I can fall into your loving arms,
into your soft embrace

Can I let go and trust that everything
will be ok and that you will
stand by my side when there is nothing left

Or will you turn your back and leave
Like love has done before

LIFE

How can you be sad
When the sky is not gray
Has this life
Made you so mad
Wish it was something
You never had

If so,
What a tragedy that is
For you only have
This one Life
So be glad

LONELY

I'm so lonely
 so, so lonely.
Loneliness
 has consumed me.
Feel as though
 it will never change.
That the storm will last forever

People pass by
 as if I don't exist.
Never stopping to say
 "Hello" or "Goodbye"

This gray road has
 gotten colder,
 more desolate.

Has the clock stopped?
Does time move slower
when you are alone?

I am so tired
of feeling lonely,
in a room full of
People.

ALIVE

There are times where it feels like a dream.
Living your life only to wake up and realize,
you really are alive.
The feeling hits you hard.
You look around the room as if everything
is foreign.
Look at your hand and realize
you exist.
You are no foreigner to this world
Not a figment of your imagination
You are not some character in a novel
Not some words written for a script

Realization hits and you begin to see
You are alive
You are the creator of your life
That you have the world
Within your grasp and that
You can create and be whomever you wish to be
You are held down by no one
But yourself
Take everything
Live everyday with hope and passion
Believing in whatever gives you life
Never settle for the bare minimum
For that is not enough
We live everyday
We die only once

Live everyday being whomever you truly are
    Believing in everything
    Never letting anyone tell you otherwise

Opening your eyes
    Its not a dream
    But a reality in which you live in
    A reality where you are alive
    A living breathing person
It truly is a weird feeling

FALL DAY

As the brisk morning air fills my lung
    I slowly open my tired dreary eyes
Darkness
    All I see is darkness
It engulfed me
    Like a blanket that was protecting me
    From the cold fall air
I sat patiently and listened
    As the breeze danced through
    The leaves of the trees
    And shook the needles of the pine
The sweet smell fills my nose
    A scent that calms ones soul after a long week
    Takes you back to a simpler time
A scent that heals
The sweet melody of the birds can be heard
    As a soft gentle stroke of blues and greens
    Begin to be painted across the early morning sky
Like a painting in an old western museum
    The birth of the light illuminates the rich dark outline
Of the sea of mountains that fade
    Into the everlasting horizon

CHRISTMAS DAY

Gone
In the way snowflakes fade
In the brisk winter wind
As the sun rises and glows
In your angelic presence

PERSEPHONE

There are some questions
That will never be answered
Feelings that will never change
Heartache and pain
That will never go away

BEAUTY OF THE MOON

Splendid is the moon
For she basks in the beauty of the sun
Never jealous
Never curses
The beauty in appreciating
The kindness of those around…
Reminds me of you

THE REALITY OF LIFE

Life is precious
Smile a lot
Cry when you need to
Forgive, even if it hurts
Always be kind to others
Live like today is your last
Love with your whole heart

Treasure everything and
everyone
you never know what
tomorrow brings
Respect others
Live life the way
you choose

IN BETWEEN

On the plain between here and there
A place where time stands still
where the sun and moon
Reign in the sky together
And flowers grow in the desolate winter
We meet

A silent moment where we stand facing each other
Snow falling all around us
The sun illuminating your hair

So close yet so far apart
Like the sun and moon
Destined to be close but
Never to embrace

You smile softly as if nothing is wrong
Your gentle presence begins to heal my
Shattered soul

Frozen in joy, I reach out to you
But when I take a step towards you;
Like a fire whose life is cut short by water
You vanish like smoke

Once again I am left alone
A prisoner to my thoughts
Trapped in my mind
Wondering if I will see you again

Or if the promise of tomorrow
Is all too sweet to be true
And the possibility of revival
Is just a lie
To draw me in

MY FOREVER MIRACLE

Time spent with you is
A true gift
My refuge in the storm
Your smiling face
Has saved me

I'd give you the world
Even if you say goodbye
I'll still be by your side

You're my heart, my soul, my world
The sun
You brighten my world
Forever want you by my side

No words I say to you
Will ever be in vain
Like sea of brilliant light
A world of hope
You're the greatest gift I could have

This moment may pass by
The sky may turn gray
But my heart won't falter
I'll be there to always hold
Your hand

You're my heart, my soul, my world
The sun
You brighten my world
Forever want you by my side

INSPIRATION

I miss you
In the way the earth
Misses the sun's warmth
On a cloudy day

Or the way flowers miss
The rain of spring
As the summer heat begins

In the way an artist
Has lost the vision
Of his masterpiece
The person of his
Momentous glory

Or the way a poet misses his music
And musician
His melody

MOMS PROMISE

The pain has come
Time to heal
Slowly but surely

It's okay to cry
Don't worry
I'll always be there
When you need me

SILENT CRY

A silent cry sounds through the night
As those who inhabit the day
Lay fast asleep, humble and timid
While she lays there, staring at the ceiling she wonders
"Why me"
Mumbling to herself as warm tears shriek down her free
Showing the hidden thoughts her heart can never say

Traveled down this place so many times
Faced giants and terrors she has overcome
Closing in on the finish line,

From out of nowhere
The world comes crashing down on her shoulders
Like Atlas she stands there
Trying to hold up
This newfound weight

Slowly inching her way home
She stumbles and falls,
Blood pouring down her hands and knees

Her breath becoming strained
Her body becoming weak
Eyes filling with tears
Her timid mind thinks about giving up
But as she looks up, she finds hope

Through the thunderous devilish storm clouds
That surround her
A bright light breaks through
A heavenly beacon to lead her to the end
Where she can win the battle

So she takes one more step forward
Following the light to the end
As that she can sleep at night
Trusting she will be alright

TO YOU

To you
The one who shines far beyond the world
Past the stars in the vast sea of the universe

May my wish find you
Let my words comfort you
Let my smile bring you
What little joy I have left
Inside of me

Know that the rain still falls
The edge of the cliff still crumbles
The skies still turn gray

But the sun has emerged
Beneath the valley of death
Giving life
Bringing warmth

Hoping that within time
It may be able to grow
The life that once resided in me
The life that was shattered
When the dawn
Led the angel to the place
Beyond the sky

FOREVERMORE

When one is finally able
to open their eyes and see
Through their foggy mistakes, their hate, their rage,
And the fires that destroy
the mind, body, and soul

They will see that behind the veil
Lies a world
They would have never imagined
A miracle in itself
This gift
Few choose to use it
This tragic twist of fate

When we mourn
What is it that really causes us grief
Is it the fact we regret something we did or didn't do
Is it a sad blessing from our loved ones
Gifting us a life that they blessed with their presence

A gift that we can never thank them enough for
Is that grief
Knowing they gave us so much
Only to have the memories of love
Forever more

SIMPLICITY

If I am drowning in my sorrows
Will you pull me to safety
If I am blinded by greed
Will you guide me back to simplicity

VALUABLE

Don't hide your eyes
The day will get better
Take my hand
Let's go and enjoy our time
Let's have fun
Come show me that smile

Your voice can soothe
The roughest seas
Your existence is
A gift of its own
So don't frown today

Whenever you are sad
Or down
Promise you will come
To me

They may walk
The other way
But the gem
That was you
Has caught my eye

Don't ever think
You're not good enough
Cause you are the
Inspiration for these
words

Don't run and hide
Don't be afraid
Cause I won't
Leave you alone

So take my hand
Lets fly to the sky
Lets see what life
Has to offer

PEACE

For the first time in a long time
I feel at peace
As if I have woken from a long sleep
And broken free from the coffin
I was trapped in

Free as a newborn
Who is breathing in their first
Breath of life
The sense of peace is unnerving
Yet thrilling
The feeling I have craved for so long

LIFE AND DEATH

I will not fear death
Nor will I try and run from it
To be able to see, grow, and flourish-
To experience, to shed tears of joy and sorrow
To feel the embrace of a loved one
And to be loved,
All of which I will cherish

And as much as I love life
I do not wish to live forever
For I fear I would take it for granted
And never truly appreciate it as a gift

When I die
I do not want people to cry
I wish for them to rejoice in remembrance of me
And then forget me
For as I once was, I am no more

Bittersweet yes but beautiful
For when I meet death
I shall meet them like a brother,
One that I had never known but wish to

A brother I could tell my story to
One whom will be excited to hear

For like life
He too has always wanted to cherish
That special gift

MY MUSE

Strength of my life
A comfort in the crippling world
We live in
The one person
I would ever call home

My muse
My everything
You are gone

You know that I am a child at heart
Immature it may be;
I need your hand to guide me
For I fear without you
I would be lost

Now that you have left
The days have grown cold
It is as if the sun
Refuses to rise again

I cannot curse you for
Not giving me a second glance
Nor can I hate myself for
Being the person who I am

For one can never give up
Whom they truly are
To do so
Would be not only an insult
To the person they are
But the person whom they care for

For the foundations of the Earth
Were created by those
Who stayed true to themselves
And not others

Tragic and as destroying as it is
I shall let you be
For I'd rather have you find the joy
And happiness that I have failed to give

Than live a hollow and empty life
That has no true meaning

LOVE EMBRACES ALL

Even if it hurts
Don't be afraid to love
Love is what gave
you this world
Love is what saved
you from this world
Love is what
cherishes you

HOME

When I look at you
I see home
I never want to lose sight
of you

MY LIGHT

You are the inspiration to my life
You are everything to me
If I am having a bad day
Seeing you smile
Makes the pain go away

Hearing you laugh
Hearing you talk
About your dreams
Brings joy to my days
Fills my weary soul
With happiness

Whenever I am down
Or need a shoulder to cry on
You were always there
Like a guardian angel
Who watches over me

You are always there
To make life better
To give life meaning
And me a purpose

I cannot find a way
To express how much
You mean to me
How much I care for you

I cannot express the lengths
I would go for you
To see you happy
To give you joy and peace

I would give my very soul
To make all your wishes come true
Your dreams a reality
I would do anything
Just to see that smile on your face
The one that made me believe
In miracles

All I can say is thank you
For being you
Staying by my side
And never leaving me
Never failing to see the light
Within me when I became blind to it

For having the courage to stand up
And defend me
When I could not fight for myself

I promise you that
I will always stand by you
I will defend you to my dying breath

I will give everything
To make sure you are happy
And that this world
That is both cruel and loving,
Treats you with the love
I have for you

It is because you
are everything to me
You are the star that
Leads me home
The water that quenches my thirst
The light to my world
I will always and forever
Love you

NIGHTINGALE

The shadow behind you
Hides your true charm
Dims the brightest star
Steals the love
From your heart

Your breath is stolen
From you
As the sun rises and
Sets each day
The life you cherished
Is crumbling at your feet

You're slowly becoming
Lost in this maze called life
Wondering when you
Will find the end

At first everything
May seem crazy
You might get confused
It may not make sense
Hold onto my words

Cause when you wake
The moon will glow
The butterflies will dance
At your feet

The skies may change
But we'll find
The place you call
Home

Do you hear the cry
Of the nightingale
A song to save you
From your nightmares
A song to cast
Your heartache away

One day we'll find
The key
The key that opens
Your heart
Until then
Spread your wings and fly
Your journey has just begun

THANK YOU

Even when I was lonely
you were there
Whenever I was sad
You made me smile

How can I thank you enough
You've helped me more times
than I could ever count
How can I ever repay you

SPECIES

In this age
we are going a million miles an hour
Our lives literally pass us by.
Repeating everything day in and out.
Our minds, bodies, and souls are connected to technology.
We live a reality that is untrue to ourselves.

Society has become so focused
On maintaining its look and
Feeding its pride
That we keep feeding into our
Bottomless ego
One that will never be full

We build ourselves a fake reality
To hide all the shame and emptiness inside
That we have grown accustomed to living
Such an unfulfilling pretentious life

One that destroys us
Little by little
Until we are nothing but a shell
A hollowed version of ourselves

Ones whose dreams and hopes
Were killed by the cruel reality
Created by those in power
Those of wealth

Hoping and praying
That the middle man may never know peace
Will always have to slave away
Never knowing what life
Really has to offer

So we continue to live our lives
In lies and falsehood
Believing that it will bring us joy
And the nurture we need to survive this world

It's so sad to see how we have crippled our species.

GLASS

I see the pain and regret
you hid inside
mask it with your words
and actions

Oh,
How you do more damage
to yourself than others
If you leave it inside
it will eventually kill you
Push people away
you'll end up
forever alone

Do these thoughts
not cross your mind
or do you not care
Cause you've been
blaming everyone
but yourself

THE WORLD IS OURS

The daylight fades into the sky
The banshee screams
Into the night
and as the choir and church
Bells sing
The gates of heaven
open before us

Twist of time
From young to old
Heartaches and heartbreaks
Forgiveness and regrets
Love and Loss
Learning to hold on
And let go

As the world collapses into ruins
Smoke fades away
And as I feel the weight of those
Who came before me
All their pain, suffering, joy, and dreams-
The pain invades my being
As it consumes the night

Angels sing hymns
Of times of long forgotten

Heroes rise from the ashes
Coming together to
Destroy the sun
That has turned black
All those years ago

Though the tragedy of mistakes
That haunt our yesterday
And blind our tomorrow,
Weigh heavily on the minds
Of the generations of man
The Angel of Death
Sees nothing but the righteous
Trying to retie the bonds
That had been destroyed

May the people of
The future never
Forget the past
Those who were the voice to some
A savior for all
The foundation of society
The hope for the world

Evolution may continue
We may never bleed out
The hate or stop
The wars and hurt that may
Eventually happen
That being said

We are what we make
We are who we decide to be
The pillars that hold the pantheon up

Letting the weight bear down on them
For they know they have the strength
To endure it and have
Nothing to fear, nothing to lose

Our dreams
Can be the hope
For tomorrow
The spark the world has been looking for
So I dare you to seek it
I challenge you to dream it
For this is the truth
The truth everyone should remember

The World Is Ours

OUTRO

From The Depths

In the valleys where giants and man
Lived in harmony
Where all creation lived as one
Where death was nothing feared
For it was never imagined-

The ancient of ancients
Resides among the sands
Which have seen the fates of man
Come and go
Time and time again

The ancient one sits quietly,
Eyes closed-
Never having opened them in
Its entire existence
For if it were to see
The world-
If it were to see it
Through the eyes of
mankind.
It would never be able

To see and believe the world
With a fair and just heart

-

Within the cave that is carved
Into the side of the
Hill that is hidden away
Amongst the valley
Of the kings

He sits in silence
The signs of the future
Layout before him
Speaking the words of
Truth to those who
Have traveled all the way
To see him

Believing in the words
That have spoken through him
From the ones from high above
The ones that were said to be
The creators of the universe
The visionaries for the human race
The ones who gave them life
Yet are the very ones
Who have stripped away
The very creations that
Give life to these beings

-

When the sun falls down
Over the horizon that sits
At the edge of the sea,
For its rest,

The darkness embodies the world
Creating an endless abyss
Of unseeing nature
Creating a cold
That bites at mans flesh

People pray and weep
And asks the spirits of the higher plane
For help, for any source of power
To give them light
To give the warmth
In this endless blanket of night

Though worshiped and loved
Having been given blessings and offerings
Those celestial beings
Bask in the glory but refuse to
Help those ones they created

One man was tired of this
Living in the dark
Humanity never able to move forward
Never flourishing in life
Always slaving away in the dirt
And only feasting on the scraps of the world

So he goes to find the source
Of what could give his people growth
On his journey he goes through trials
And things that seem impossible for any
Other human but not to him

Finally he obtained it
Obtained the sacred glow
That gives the people
The strength and ability
To move forward
And better themselves

-

As beautiful as it is
For someone to do something
To help the people
And give them hope for
The future

It was seen as crime
As sin against the Gods
The ones that gave life
But not the tools to survive

For reasons man will never understand
Theses beings grew angry
And captured this man
And choose a punishment for him
A punishment that shall forever
Go on
Though it is painful
Though he withers in agony
He smiles
The man smiles for he knows
That these beings are jealous
Jealous because he did something
That they never believed was possible

He did it for no glory
No payment

No offerings
He did it to better mankind
Something the Gods could never understand

-

Those who say the lies and deception
The ones that say clarity through
The wicked grins
Were struck down
Erased from history

Some were cursed
Forced to live forever
To watch their loved ones
Fade away one by one
Nothing they do
Could ever let them see them again

Cursed to be like the ones
They so righteously object
The beings that are unjust in every way imaginable

How is it they could find justice
In destroying and silencing those
Who fight for justice
Who fight for the right to live

When they themselves
Fight for glory and honor
And for the sake of glorifying themselves
As the superior beings

They forsake the ones
Who work so hard and sacrifice
Everything for others

They only ever help
When they know it will benefit them

The fate of humanity
Does not rest in the hands
Of any God or any higher being
Not the hands of mankind
Or the decisions he makes

No,
It is determined by how far
One is willing to go
In order to better the world
With no desire for recognition
No desire for praise

The act of selflessness
Is what keeps the world at bay
And all the scales in balance

The ancient of ancient
Having told the masses
The visions of the past and future
Now rises, the bones of its weary body
Creaking with every move
Slowly and silently
He leaves the shelter of his home

As he steps into the sun
The light illuminates his
Sickening look
The last few pieces of his cloak
Barely held together

The people of the village that
Resides far beyond his home
Watch in silence
As they marvel at the sight
That lies before them

Never,
In the generations that have lived
In this area
Never had they ever seen the man
Step outside

The cursed one
The last of his kind
A man that had stood with the gods
And walked among the bravest men
The one that stood before everyone
And renounced his humanity before
The ones that created him

As his breath begins to grow slow
He trudges through the sand
The winds blowing hot air
Into his face
His hood falling down
And giving warmth
To the face that has become
So sunken
It looked as though it was
The very face of death itself

Having reached the very top
Of the hill
He lived under for eons
He lifts his head to the sky
And raises his arm

Then he laughs
He laughs as he
Mocks the ones who made him this way
For despite the centuries of pain
The agony of having to live alone
Foretelling others futures and dreams
So that they may have hope
Nothing really was a curse

For a curse is but a punishment
A punishment that was given
To someone for something they did
Something that someone believed
Was wrong
Something they did not agree with

Yet the ancient of ancients
Did not see it this way
He saw it as nothing short of a joke
For when the gods stripped away
His humanity
And he was forced to become one
With them
They failed to take away
The very thing that makes a person
Human

Selflessness

ABOUT THE AUTHOR

Hi! My name is Piper Lawson and I'm a small author from North Idaho. I have always had a love for poetry and writing because it allows me to write my experiences and feelings in a way that might reach others and to help them. I've always enjoyed writing, music, and all things creative.

Printed in the USA
CPSIA information can be obtained
at www.ICGtesting.com
LVHW022230090524
779584LV00004B/316

9 781637 843970